HAPPY WOM

THE MERRY LADY

TURN BACK THE CLOCK AND REDISCOVER YOUR YOUTH ONCE AGAIN

Jennifer Hall

Table of Contents

PART 1 5

Chapter 1: *What Every Successful Person Knows, but Never Says*.....6

Chapter 2: Happy People Stay Present..................................9

Chapter 3: Friendship The Key To Happiness 15

Chapter 4: The Magic of the 5 Minute Rule 18

Chapter 5: Consistency can bring you happiness................20

Chapter 6: 10 Habits of Happy People 24

Chapter 7: Happy People Are Proactive About Relationships.............29

Chapter 8: Consistency 32

Chapter 9: 10 Habits to Change Your Life.......................35

Chapter 10: Becoming a Leader 42

PART 2 45

Chapter 1: Achieving Happiness 46

Chapter 2: The Only Obstacle Is Yourself 48

Chapter 3: Fight Lethargy and Win 53

Chapter 4: Twenty Percent of Effort Produces 80% of Results 57

Chapter 5: Happy People Choose to Exercise 59

Chapter 6: 8 Ways To Love Yourself First......................61

Chapter 7: Happy People Spend Time Alone 66

Chapter 8: *Overcome Demotivation* 69

Chapter 9: Happy People Surround Themselves with The Right People
....72

Chapter 10: Happy People Live Slow.............................75

PART 3 77

Chapter 1: How To Worry Less 78

Chapter 2: Happy People Do What Matters to Them............81

Chapter 3: Pressures of Social Media 86

Chapter 4: Do You Know What You Want? 89

Chapter 5: *7 Ways On How To Attract Success In Life* 92

Chapter 6: 6 Steps To Focus On Growth 96

Chapter 7: 6 Tricks To Become More Aware Of Your Strengths 101

Chapter 8: Seven Habits of Mentally Strong People 106

Chapter 9: *5 Scientific Tricks To Become Perfectly Happy* 111

Chapter 10: 8 Habits That Can Make You Happy 115

Conclusion 119

PART 1

Chapter 1:

What Every Successful Person Knows, but Never Says

Every person you meet will have a slightly different definition of what success is to them. Whether the goal is centered around finance, health, relationships, or their career, the point of "Success" is subjective. No matter what it looks like.. we all desire to achieve it in one way or another. We desire to achieve, excel, and gain; this is just a part of human nature.

When we decide to reach for success or set ourselves a new goal, it's obvious that at the point we are at, we have less understanding, knowledge, or skills than someone who has already reached that goal.

So it can be said that when we set a goal, we not only set a challenge to achieve something specific, we set ourselves a challenge to become the person who can achieve that thing. We do this through gaining new skills, practice and determination.

What Every Successful Person Knows but You Won't Hear Them Say

Often when we are at the starting point of attempting to achieve something new, a goal can feel overwhelming. We can feel as though the goal itself is HUGE or that perhaps we aren't capable of achieving it at all.

But the thing about success is that it's a process.

Malcolm Gladwell's book Outliers stated that it takes 10,000 hours of practice to become a master of something. This is a theory, of course, which will vary from person to person, but the point is clear. There is no such thing as overnight success. It takes years to become successful.

People generally don't talk about this part of becoming successful. Maybe because most of us don't want to hear the reality. In a world of instant gratification, perhaps the idea of long-term hard work is too difficult to swallow. The truth is, not only does it take years to become successful at something, but at the beginning of your journey, you're probably going to suck at it.

Yep. There will likely be a bunch of time, be it days, weeks, months, or years of you learning to be great at something that you simply won't be any good at. This is partly why many people never try new things. The idea of not being immediately brilliant at something is too much for their ego to bear.

It's kind of sad to think about how many people never try anything new or set themselves a goal because they feel like they need to be good straight away.

You Don't!

You can't! It's completely necessary not to be good at some stuff. How will you grow and evolve and get better at anything if you don't suck a little bit to start with?

Chapter 2:
Happy People Stay Present

"Realize deeply that the present moment is all you ever have."

According to a study, 50% of the time, we are not fully present in the moment. We are either thinking about the past or worrying about the future. These things lead to frustration, anxiety, and pain in our daily life. Each morning as soon as we wake up, we start seeking distractions. As we wake up with a clear mind, we should be grateful for a new day that we got; instead, we start looking for our phone, start going through interwebs and rush into our days. So now we are going to help you and list some of the things that will help you stay present.

Stop Being a Slave to Your Mind: For the next four days, let's do an exercise where you pay attention to your thoughts and see what crosses your mind. You. You will soon realize that majority of the thoughts that you have are destructive. There will be very little time to think about the present, and the majority of your thoughts would be about the past or the future. So, whenever this happens and you find yourself wandering consciously, try to bring yourself back to the present. Also, you need to remind yourself that multi-tasking is a myth and focus on one thing only.

Tap into Your Senses: If you mindfully tap into your senses, you will realize that it is a fantastic way of bringing more awareness into your day. Because our eyes are wide open all day, we can see, but we forget to tap into other senses such as taste, touch, or smell. But if you use these, you can feel more present and calm down if you are in a stressful situation. You might not realize this, but our senses play a huge role in manifesting our reality. For example, everything we are hearing we are touching will regularly turn into our reality. That is why we can use the power our senses have and feel more calm and present.

Listen Closely: Everyone loves to talk, but only a few people like to listen. People love to share their dreams, what they have accomplished and what they desire, and still, nobody seems to be listening closely.

"When you talk, you are only repeating what you already know. But if you listen, you may learn something new."

When you listen carefully, you will be able to charm people and at the same time learn new things and be present. Because you will be focusing on what they are saying, you will focus on the current moment. This way, you will also be able to silence your thoughts about the past and future because you will be consciously listening and focusing on what they are saying. This will also benefit your relationship in the long run because when you need an ear to listen to your problems, they will be there for you. This is a win-win situation for you, and you will improve your relationship while practising being more present.

Happy People Use Their Character Strengths

One of the most popular exercises in the science of positive psychology (some argue it is the single most popular exercise) is referred to as "use your signature strengths in new ways." But what does this exercise mean? How do you make the most of it to benefit yourself and others?

On the surface, the exercise is self-explanatory:

a. Select one of your highest strengths – one of your **character strengths** that is core to who you are, is easy for you to use, and gives you energy;

b. Consider a new way to express the strength each day;

c. Express the strength in a new way each day for at least 1 week.

Studies repeatedly show that this exercise is connected with long-term benefits (e.g., 6 months) such as higher levels of happiness and lower levels of depression.

PUT THE EXERCISE INTO PRACTICE

In practice, however, people sometimes find it surprisingly challenging to come up with new ways to use one of their signature strengths. This is because we are very accustomed to using our strengths. We frequently use our strengths mindlessly without much awareness. For example, have you paid much attention to your use of self-regulation as you brush your teeth? Your level of prudence or kindness while driving? Your humility while at a team meeting?

For some strengths, it is easy to come up with examples. Want to apply **curiosity** in a new way? Below is a sample mapping of what you might do. Keep it simple. Make it complex. It's up to you!

- On Monday, take a new route home from work and explore your environment as you drive.
- On Tuesday, ask one of your co-workers a question you have not previously asked them.
- On Wednesday, try a new food for lunch – something that piques your curiosity to taste.
- On Thursday, call a family member and explore their feelings about a recent positive experience they had.
- On Friday, take the stairs instead of the elevator and explore the environment as you do.
- On Saturday, as you do one household chore (e.g., washing the dishes, vacuuming), pay attention to 3 novel features of the activity while you do it. Example: Notice the whirring sound of the vacuum, the accumulation of dust swirling around in the container, the warmth of the water as you wash the dishes, the sensation of the weight of a single plate or cup, and so on.
- On Sunday, ask yourself 2 questions you want to explore about yourself – reflect or journal your immediate responses.
- Next Monday….keep going!

WIDENING THE SCOPE

In some instances, you might feel challenged to come up with examples. Let me help. After you choose one of your signature strengths, consider the following 10 areas to help jolt new ideas within you and stretch your approach to the strength.

How might I express the character strength…

- At work
- In my closest relationship
- While I engage in a hobby
- When with my friends
- When with my parents or children
- When I am alone at home
- When I am on a team
- As the leader of a project or group
- While I am driving
- While I am eating

Chapter 3:
Friendship The Key To Happiness

Today we're going to talk about the power of friendship and why i believe everyone needs to have at least 1 or 2 close friends in their lives to make life actually meaningful and worth living.

You see, for many years while i was working hard towards my goals, i spent almost all of my time on my business and little to zero time on building Long lasting relationships. And this one sided approach to success left me with a hole that weakened me emotionally, but also physically as well.

In this very myopic view of what I felt success should be and what I felt i needed to do at that point, I prioritised my career first over everything else, neglecting my own personal health, family, and friends. Whenever I was invited for a meal or an outing I always declined, viewing that it was a waste of time. That it was taking time away from my work that i should be focusing on. And as I declined more and more of these offers from friends, the invite also became less and less frequent as they saw me as someone who was either too busy, or just didn't bother to want to take this friendship to the next level.

For a while I was actually happy, that i remember telling myself that yes I dont have plans for the week and that i can focus on my work wholeheartedly. But what i failed to realise was that I was prioritise making money over everything else. And that i was losing the connection with other humans. I started to become more withdrawn, more introverted, and I was losing that spark that i once had when conversing with friends. I wasn't experiencing life enough to have any meaningful moments that I could look back on and say that wow those were great times.

The Merry Lady

It all became one giant blur and 3 years later, it felt truly pointless. I found myself lonely and without someone I could talk to. I even neglected my best friend to the point that we drifted so far apart that she found other people to confide into. This left me with a sinking feeling that I had failed to prioritise The people around me.

And from that point on I knew i needed to change. I knew i needed to put myself out there once again and shift my priorities to the things that truly mattered. Friends that could ask you out for a quick meal so that you could hash out some of your grievances in life, friends that you can share your happiness as well as your sadness, friends that could provide some meaning to the days you were living, and even more simply, friends that you can count on when all else fails.

You see the business that I spent 3 years building collapsed on me. And I found myself with nothing to show for it. No experiences worth highlighting. Only regrets that I had failed to put others before my selfish needs.

It was a hard climb back to establishing the friendships I once had. People had already started viewing me as a flaker and a no-show that it was now up to me to prove to them that I was open and available to be called a reliable friend once again. Some efforts on my part did not go as I had planned but I kept trying to make new connections, joining new groups, making tennis friends, starting up conversations with new people and asking if they could invite me along to an outing. And these little seeds started to show fruition. I soon found myself getting asked out for meals and games, and life started to feel a little bit better again.

After the initial struggle, the floodgates starting opening and I found myself busy with true life again, connecting with other people on a deep personal and emotional level. And i felt that that was what life was really all about. Friends that you can see yourself hanging out 40 years down the road when you are old and nobody wants you anymore.

The Merry Lady

I plan to keep sowing these seeds for as long as life allows me and I challenge each and everyone of you to do the same. Businesses and careers may not last, but hopefully the friends that you have made will.

Take care and I'll see you in the next one.

Chapter 4:

The Magic of the 5 Minute Rule

Recently I have been struggling to get things done, more so than usual. It has become a daily battle with myself to sit down on my desk to begin the necessary work that I know i need to do. However looking at the endless list of tasks i have in front of me, i can't help but to choose procrastination and slacking over beginning my work. And it has affected my ability to be a productive member of society.

Whilst I knew in the back of my mind that I believe the work that I do can benefit society, and that it has the power to give me freedom of time and money to get and do the things that i really wanted to do in life, on some level it wasn't actually enough to get me to start the work. Many a times I felt really sluggish and it would take some strong reminders to get me motivated enough to start the work. That was the point where i decided i needed to search for a solution that work not only make work more enjoyable, but to also push me to get work started much faster without delay.

After spending some solid hours researching, i came across one strategy that I felt would work like a charm on me. And that is to employ the 5 minute rule to every single task that I have on hand.

The biggest problem that I have currently is that I am working on 10 different projects at any one time. And when I look at these 10 separate projects that need my attention, I can't help but feel overwhelmed about the number of hours that I needed to schedule for each of these projects. And that seemed like a mountainous task for me to climb. And looking at it as a whole, it felt absolutely daunting and impossible. Which was what made me not want to even attempt to begin that climb.

The Merry Lady

How the 5 minute rule works is that for every project that I needed to work on, I wrote that I only needed to do the task for 5 minutes. However ridiculous that sounded, it actually worked like a charm. My brain was tricked into thinking that this became much more manageable and i would accomplish it easily. And we all know that the biggest problem is getting started. But once u do, you tend to keep going. And so for every task that i told myself i needed to do for 5 minutes, in reality i ended up spending the adequate amount of time i needed to do to get the job done. whether it be 10 minutes, 30minutes, an hour, or even several hours.

I managed to trick my brain into breaking each project down to its most basic manageable form and that gave me to confidence that I could crush it with ease. I applied this technique to not only work, but also going to the gym, walking my dog, and other administrative and personal tasks that I was lazy to do. And i saw my ability to begin each task and eventually check it off my to-do list increase exponentially. My productivity level also skyrocketed as a result.

With this simple trick in your arsenal. I believe anyone that you too can begin your work much quicker as well and crush every single task that will be put in front of you today and in your future. So i challenge each and everyone of you today to just tell yourself that you will only need to set aside 5 mins for each task and see where that takes you, and that I believe will be in the right direction.

Chapter 5:
Consistency can bring you happiness.

Happiness is an individual concept.

One man's riches is another man's rubbish.

As humans we are not happy if we do not have a routine, a reason to get up, and a purpose to live.

Without working towards something consistently, we become lost.

We begin to drift.

Drifting with no purpose eventually leads to emptiness.

When we are drifting in a job we hate,

We are trading our future away,

When we inconsistent in our relationships,

Problems are bound to arise.

Choose consistent focus instead.

Figure out exactly what you want and start to change it.

Employ consistent routines and habits that to move you towards your goals.

Consistency and persistence are key to success and happiness.

Without consistent disciplined effort towards what we want, we resign to a life of mediocrity.

Read a book for an hour consistently every single day.

You will become a national expert in 1 year.

In 5 years, a global expert.

That is the power of consistency.

The Merry Lady

Instead, people spend most of their free time scrolling through social media.

Consistency starts in the mind.
Control your thoughts to be positive despite the circumstances.
Nothing in the world can make us happy if we choose not to be.

Choose to be happy now and consistently working towards your goals.
We cannot be happy and successful if we dwell in the day to day setbacks.

We must consistently move like a bulldozer.
We have to keep going no matter what.
Nothing stays in the path of a bulldozer for too long.

In life, no matter where you are, you only ever have two choices.
Choose to stay where you are? Or choose to keep moving?

If where you are is making you happy, then by all means do more of it.
If not. What will? And why?
This should be clear before you take action.
Start with the end in your mind.
Let your body catch-up to it afterwards.
The end result is your what.
The action required is your how.
Concentrate on the what and the how and it will all be revealed soon enough.

Concentrate consistently on what you want for yourself and your family.
Distraction and lack of consistent action is a killer of happiness and success.
Your happiness is the life you want.
Take consistent action towards that life you've always dreamed of.
Commitment and endurance is part of that process.

On earth things need time to nurture and grow.

The Merry Lady

Everything in life depends on it.

The right conditions for maximum growth.

You can't just throw a seed on the concrete and expect it to grow with no soil and water, Just as you can't simply wish for change and not create the right environment for success.

A seed requires not just consistent sunlight,

But the perfect combination of water and nutrients as well.

You might have given that seed sunlight,

just as you have your dream hope,

But without faith and consistent action towards the goal, nothing will happen.

The seed will still stay a seed forever.

Consistency in thought and action is everything towards happiness.

Nothing can grow without it.

Your success can be measured by your time spent working towards your goals.

If we consistently do nothing we become successful in nothing.

If we have to do something, should it not be something worth doing?

Start doing things that make you happy and fulfilled.

Consistency towards something that makes you happy is key towards lasting success.

Adapt when necessary but remain consistent with the end result in mind.

The path can be changed when necessary but the destination cannot.

Accepting anything less is admitting defeat.

Consistent concentration on the end result can and will be tested.

It however cannot be defeated, unless you quit.

If we remain steadfast in our belief that this is possible for us, it will be possible.

After a while things will seem probable. Eventually it becomes definite.

Continue to believe you can do it despite the circumstances.

The Merry Lady

Continue despite everyone around you saying you can't do it.

In spite of social status,
in spite of illness or disability,
in spite of age, race or nationality,
know you can do nearly anything if you consistently put all of your mind and body towards the task.

Take the pressure off.
There is no set guideline.
It is what you make of it.

There is no set destination or requirements.
Those are set my you.

The only competition is yourself from yesterday.
If you can consistently outperform that person, your success is guaranteed.
Consistent concentration and action towards your dream is key you your success and happiness.

Chapter 6:

<u>10 Habits of Happy People</u>

Happy people live the most satisfying lives on the planet. They have come to understand the importance of not worrying because it will not make any differential change in their lives. If you cannot control the outcome of a process, why worry? If you can control and make a difference to the outcome of a situation, why worry? Worrying does not bring an ounce of success your way.

Here are 10 habits of happy people that could be you if you choose to adopt it:

1. <u>Happy People Count Their Blessings.</u>

Taking stock of your successes is an important part of appreciating yourself. You find comfort in knowing that despite all the hiccups you have found in your journey there remains an oasis of achievements in your desert.

Everyone needs to take stock of what is in his or her basket of blessings. It is a reminder of your resilience and persistence in the face of challenges. It is an indication of your ability and a minute representation of the progress you can make, given time.

Remind yourself of the taste of victory in your small achievements. It begins with understanding that you definitely cannot be able to win it all. There are grey and shadow areas that will not be within your reach.

2. Happy People Do Not Need the Validation of Others.

Happy people do not wait for the validation of other people. They are autonomous. Develop the habit of doing what is right regardless of your audience and you will have an authentic lifestyle. As such, your source of happiness will be independent of uncontrollable factors. Why should you tie your happiness to someone else capable of ruining your day in a snap? This is not to mean that you will not need other people. Humans are social beings and interdependent. Letting them strongly influence your lifestyle is the major problem. Be your own man.

3. They Are Bold.

Boldly and cautiously pursuing their ambitions is part of the ingredients that make up happy people. Knowing what you want is one thing and pursuing it is another. If music is your passion and it makes you happy, chase after it for it is therein that your happiness lies. Whatever it is (of course considering its legality) do not let it pass.

To be truly happy, do not live in the shadow of other happy people. Define your happiness and drink from your well. Timidity will make you bask under the shade of giants and create a sense of false security. One day the shade will be no more and leave you exposed to an unimaginable reality.

4. They are social people.

Being social is one common characteristic of happy people. Happiness makes them bubbly and alive. There is a common testament in almost all happy people – either happiness made them social or their social nature made them happy. Thanks to whichever of the two came earlier, they are happy people!

Like bad luck, happiness is contagious. Your social circle can infect you with happiness or even deny it to you. Being sociable does not mean to the extreme nature with all the hype that comes along.

It means being approachable to people. Some will positively add to your basket and others will offer positive criticism towards your cause. With such input, your happiness will have longevity.

5. <u>Believe in a greater cause.</u>

Happy people understand that it is not always about them. There is a greater cause above their interests. They do not derive their happiness from the satisfaction of their needs and wants. Regardless of any deficiency in their lives, their flame of happiness is not easily put out.

Do you want to be happy? It is time to put self-interest aside and not tie your happiness to local anchors. An average person's happiness is mainly dependent on his well-being. Refusing to be average gives you leverage over those out to put off your happiness.

6. <u>Lead a purposeful life.</u>

Are there happy people without purpose? Those we see happy maintain their status by having a powerful drive towards the same. A strong purpose will make you stay on happiness' lane. It is the habit of happy people to have a purpose. This is to enable them to stay on course.

Being happy is not a permanent state. It is easily reversible if caution is not taken. Purposefulness is part of the caution taken by happy people.

7. Admit they are human.

To err is human. Given this, happy people appreciate the erroneous nature of man and accept the things they cannot change, have the courage to change the things they can, and the wisdom to know the difference. A prayer commonly referred to as the serenity prayer.

Admitting being human is the first step towards being happy. You forgive yourself of your wrongs before seeking the forgiveness of another. This brings inner peace culminating in happiness.

8. Know their strengths and weaknesses.

Being aware of your strengths and weaknesses is one thing happy people have mastered. Through that, they know their limits; the time to push and time to take a break. This serves to help avoid unwarranted disappointments that come along with new challenges.

Nothing can put off the charisma of a prepared spirit. Happy people know their limitations well enough such that no ill-willed voice can whisper disappointments to them. They hold the power of self-awareness within their hearts making them live with contentment.

9. Notice the contributions of those around them.

No man is an island. The contributions of other people in our lives cannot be emphasized enough. We are because they are (for all the good reasons). At any one point in our lives, someone made us happy. The first step is noticing the roles played by those in our immediate environment.

The joy of being surrounded by people to hold our hands in life is engraved deeper in our hearts in times of need. It is time you stop looking far away and turn your eyes to see what is next to you.

10. They are grateful and appreciative.

"Thank you" is a word that does not depart from the lips of happy people. Their hearts are trained to focus on what is at their disposal instead of what they cannot reach. It is crystal that a bird in hand is worth two in the bush.

Happy people continue being happy despite deficiencies. Try being appreciative and see how happiness will tow along.

Adopt these 10 habits of happy people and depression will keep away from you. If you want to be happy, do what happy people do and you will see the difference.

Chapter 7:
Happy People Are Proactive About Relationships

Researchers have found that as human beings we are only capable of maintaining up to 150 meaningful relationships, including five primary, close relationships.

This holds true even with the illusion of thousands of "friends" on social media platforms such as Facebook, Instagram, and Twitter. If you think carefully about your real interactions with people, you'll find the five close/150 extended relationships rule holds true.

Perhaps not coincidentally, Tony Robbins, the personal development expert, and others argue that your attitudes, behavior, and success in life are the sum total of your five closest relationships. So, toxic relationships, toxic life.

With this in mind, it's essential to continue to develop relationships that are positive and beneficial. **But in today's distracted world, these relationships won't just happen.**

We need to be proactive about developing our relationships.

My current favorite book on personal development is Tim Ferriss's excellent, though long, 700+ page book, *Tools of Titans: The Tactics, Routines, and Habits of Billionaires, Icons, and World-Class Performers.*

At one point, Ferriss quotes retired women's volleyball great Gabby Reece:

I always say that I'll go first…. That means if I'm checking out at the store, I'll say "hello" first. If I'm coming across somebody and make eye contact, I'll smile first. [I wish] people would experiment with that in their life a little bit: be first, because – not all times, but most times – it comes in your favor... The response is pretty amazing…. I was at the park the other day with the kids.

Oh, my God. Hurricane Harbor [water park]. It's like hell. There were these two women a little bit older than me. We couldn't be more different, right? And I walked by them, and I just looked at them and smiled. The smile came to their face so instantly. They're ready, but you have to go first because now we're being trained in this world [to opt out] – nobody's going first anymore.

Be proactive: start the conversation

I agree. I was excited to read this principle because I adopted this by default years ago, and it's given me the opportunity to hear the most amazing stories and develop the greatest relationships you can imagine.

On airplanes, in the grocery store, at lunch, I've started conversations that led to trading heartfelt stories, becoming friends, or doing business together. A relationship has to start someplace, and that can be any place in any moment.

Be proactive: lose your fear of being rejected

I also love this idea because it will help overcome one of the main issues I hear from my training and coaching clients – the fear of making an initial connection with someone they don't know.

This fear runs deep for many people and may be hardwired in humans. We are always observing strangers to determine if we can trust them – whether they have positive or dangerous intent.

In addition, **we fear rejection. Our usual negative self-talk says something like,** *If I start the conversation, if I make eye contact, if I smile, what if it's not returned?*

What if I'm rejected, embarrassed, or ignored by no response? I'll feel like an idiot, a needy loser.

Chapter 8:

Consistency

Today we're going to talk about a very important topic that I believe is one of the core principles that we should all strive to integrate into our lives. And that is consistency.

What does consistency mean to you when you hear that word? For me previously when I kept hearing people say that I would need to stay consistent in this and that, it did not ring any bells in me and i brushed it off thinking it was just another productivity word similar to work hard, be positive and so on. However it was only when I start doing more digging that I realized that many successful people in life actually attributed consistency as being the key factor that led to their success. That it was that one quality they possessed in their work ethic that allowed them to surpass their competition. That they had set out a plan and stuck to it consistency over days, months, years, and even decades until they finally achieved their goals.

You see for many of us, consistency is something that i believe we all struggle with. Whether it be going to the gym, putting in the effort to work out, going for trainings, health wise or work related, studying, practicing an instrument, especially things we find to be not so enjoyable to do, we just do not show up consistently enough to produce results that are satisfactory let alone ones that we are proud of. And we complain that our body doesn't look good, that we are getting nowhere with learning a new instrument, or maybe that we have plateaued in the area that we most wish to desire to move forward in, work or play.

You see, your level of consistency is directly correlated with the amount of time you actually spend on an activity. And if your consistency drops, it is no wonder that your performance drops as well as you are not putting in the adequate amount of time to

The Merry Lady

actually progress forward. As the saying goes, practice makes perfect. And Practice takes time. And time requires consistency.

Highly successful figures in any field, be it sports or the business world, from roger Federer, Lionel Messi, Michael jordan, Kobe Bryant, to Elon Musk, Bill Gates, Steve Jobs, they possess a strong vision for themselves and their consistency is a tool for their success. They would not hesitate to put every ounce of their time and energy into being the best in their field by showing up every single day for practice or for work, to get better each day and to crush their opinion. What they lack in skill, they make up for in consistency in practice. And they improve much faster than their opponents as a result, keeping them at the very top level of their game.

With the knowledge that consistency was the key to success for many entrepreneurs and businessmen, i decided to try it out for myself. Previously I was erratic in my work schedule. I always wandered around my tasks and never put in the effort to put in a set number of hours every day. I felt that my body wasn't getting any fitter, my tennis was average at best, and my income never really went anywhere. In all areas of my life, it felt like i had reached a ceiling.

After making the change to becoming more consistent in everything that I did, I saw a marked improvement in all areas that I had struggled with previously. My body started taking shape, my tennis game improved, and my income grew as well. The thing is, i hadn't done anything different apart from making it a daily habit and routine of putting in more hours into each task, showing up for more gym sessions, showing up for more tennis games, showing up for more hours at work, and consistently putting out more content. While gradual, these hours slowly added up and I saw a breakthrough. And I was surprised at how one small little change in how I approached life actually benefited me. I felt happier that i was improving in all these areas, and it had a snowball effect of actually compounding over time. Sooner or later i was beating my peers in all areas that I was once level with.

The Merry Lady

I challenge each and everyone of you to make consistency one of your core philosophies in life. To approach each and every task, project, or mission you embark on with a level of consistency unmatched by those around you. I am sure you will be very surprised at what you can achieve with just this one simple tweak in everything that you do.

I hope you learned something today and I wish you all the success in the world. Take care and I'll see you in the next one.

Chapter 9:

10 Habits to Change Your Life

I'm sure everyone wonders at a certain point in their life that what is the thing that is stopping them from reaching their goals. It is your bad and unhealthy habits that hold you down. If you want to succeed in life, you need to get rid of these habits and adopt healthy habits to help you in the long run.

Here are 10 healthy habits that will change your life completely if you can adopt them in your daily life:

Start Following a Morning Ritual

Everyone has something that they love to do, i.e., things that boost their energy and uplifts their mood. Find one for yourself and do that every morning. It will help you kickstart your day with a bright and cheerful mood. It will also help you to eliminate mental fatigue and stress. You will find yourself super energetic and productive. Let me tell you some morning rituals that you can try and get benefitted from.

Eating Healthy: If you are very passionate about health and fitness, eating healthy as a morning ritual might be a win-win situation for you. You can have a nutritious breakfast every morning. Balance your breakfast with proper amounts of carbs, fats, proteins, etc. It will not only help you in staying healthy but will also help you kickstart your day on a proactive note.

Meditating: Meditation is an excellent way of clearing your mind, enhancing your awareness, and improving your focus. You can meditate for 20 to 30 minutes every morning. Then you can take a nice warm shower, followed by a fresh cup of coffee. Most importantly, meditating regularly will also help you strengthen your immune system, promote emotional stability, and reduce stress.

Motivating: A daily dose of motivation can work wonders for you. When you are motivated, your productivity doubles, and you make the best out of your day. Every morning, you can simply ask yourself questions like, "If it is the last day of your life, what do you want to do?", "What productive thing can I do today to make the best out of the day" "What do I need to do in order to avoid regretting later for having wasted a day?". When you ask yourself questions like these, you are actually instructing your brain to be prepared for having a packed-up and productive day.

Writing: Writing can be a super-effective way of kickstarting your day. When you journal all your thoughts and emotions every day after waking up, it allows you to relieve yourself from all the mental clutter, unlocks your creative side, and sharpens your focus.

Working Out: Working out is a great morning ritual that you can follow every day. When you work out daily, it helps you burn more fat, improves your blood circulation, and boosts your energy level. If you are interested in fitness and health, this is the perfect morning ritual for you. You can do some cardio exercises, or some strength training, or both. Depending on your suitability, create a workout routine for yourself and make sure to stick to that. If you don't stick to your routine, it won't be of much help.

1. Start Following the 80/20 Rule

The 80/20 rule states that almost 20% of the tasks you perform are responsible for yielding 80% of the results. It is why you should invest more time in tasks that can give you more significant results instead of wasting your time on tasks that yield little to no results. In this way, you can not only save time but also maximize your productivity. Most importantly, when you see the results after performing those tasks, you will be more motivated to complete the following tasks. After you have finished performing these tasks, now you can quickly move your concentration and focus towards other activities that you need to do throughout your day.

2. Practice Lots of Reading

Reading is a great habit and a great way to stimulate your creativity and gaining more knowledge. When you get immersed in reading, it calms you and improves your focus, almost similar to meditating. If you practice reading before going to bed, you are going to have a fantastic sleep. You can read non-fiction books, which help you seek motivation, develop new ideas, and broaden your horizon. You can also get a lot of advice about how to handle certain situations in life.

3. Start Single-tasking

Multitasking is hard, and almost 2% of the world's total population can do this properly. You can try multitasking occasionally. If you keep on trying to do this all the time, it will form a mental clutter, and as a result, your brain won't be able to filter out unnecessary information. Many studies have suggested that it can severely damage your cognitive control and lower your efficiency when you multitask a lot. It is the main reason why you should try to do single-tasking more than multitasking. Prepare a list of all the tasks you need to perform in a day and start with the most important one. Make sure not to rush and to complete one thing at a time.

4. Start Appreciating More

Appreciating things is totally dependent on your mentality. For example, some people can whine and complain about a glass being half empty, whereas some people appreciate that there is half a glass of water. It totally depends on your point of view and way of thinking. People get blinded by the urge to reach success so much that they actually forget to appreciate the little things in life. If you are working and earning a handsome salary, don't just sit and complain about why you are not earning more, what you need to do to achieve that, etc. You should obviously aim high, but not at the cost of your well-being. When you practice gratitude, it increases your creativity, improves your physical health, and reduces your stress. You can start writing about the things you are grateful for in your journal every day before going to bed, make some time for appreciating your loved ones, or remind yourself of all the things you are grateful for before going to bed every day. If you are not happy with your current situation, you will not be happy in the future. You need to be happy and satisfied at first, and then only you can work on progressing further.

5. Always Keep Positive People Around You

When you have toxic people around you, it gets tough for you to stay in a good mood or achieve something good in life. Toxic people always find a way to pull you down and make you feel bad about yourself. You should always surround yourself with people who are encouraging and positive. When you do that, your life is going to be full of positivity.

6. Exercise on a Regular Basis

Start exercising regularly to maintain good health and enhancing your creativity and cognitive skills. It also increases your endurance level and boosts your energy. When you exercise regularly, your body produces more endorphins. These hormones work as anti-depressants.

7. Start Listening More

Effective communication is very important in maintaining both professional and personal relationships. For communicating effectively, you need to work on your listening capability first. You need to pay attention to the things said by others instead of focusing only on what you have to say. Listening to others will allow you to understand them better. When you listen to someone, it makes them understand that they are valued and that you are here to listen to them. When they feel important and valued, they also start paying attention to what you say, thereby contributing to effective communication. Don't try to show fake concentration while you are busy thinking about something else. When you listen more, you learn more.

8. Take a Break from Social Media (Social Media Detox)

Many studies have shown that excessive use of social media can contribute to depression. Most importantly, it wastes a lot of time because people meaninglessly scroll, swipe, and click for hours. It is a very unhealthy habit and is very bad for bothe physical and mental health. Sometimes you need to completely stop using social media for a while to reduce mental clutter and stress. Turn off your laptops and phones every day for a few hours. It will help you to reconnect with the surrounding world and will uplift your mood.

9. Start Investing More in Self-care

Make some time for yourself out of your busy schedule. It is going to boost your self-esteem, improve your mental health, and uplift your mood. You need to do at least one thing for yourself every day that will make you feel pampered and happy. You can prepare a mouth watering meal, take a comfortable bubble bath, learn something new, or just relax while listening to music.

The moment you start introducing these habits in your daily, you will instantly see change. Remember that even a tiny step towards a positive change can give outstanding results if you stay consistent.

Chapter 10:
Becoming a Leader

Wow today we're going to talk about a topic that i think might not apply to everybody but it is one that is definitely interesting as well and good for everyone to know if they some day aspire to be a leader of sorts.

Leadership is something that does not come naturally to everyone, while some are born leaders as they say, in reality most of us requires life experiences, training, and simply good people skills in order to be an effective leader that is respected.

To be a respected leader, you have to have excellent communication skills who come across as fair and just to your employees while also being able to make tough decisions when the time comes.

I believe that leaders are not born, but their power is earned. A person who has not had the opportunities to deal with others on a social and business level can never be able to make effective decisions that serves the well being of others. A leader in any organisation is one that is able to command respect not by force but by implicit authority.

So what are some ways that you can acquire leadership skills if you feel that you lack experience in it? Well first of all i believe that putting yourself in more social and group settings in friendly situations is a good place to start. Instead of jumping right into a work project, you can start by organising an activity where you are in charge. For example those that involve team work and team games. Maybe an escape room, or even simply taking charge by organising a party and planning an event where you become the host, and that usually means that you are in charge of getting things in order and all the nitty gritty stuff. Planning parties, coordinating people, time management, giving instructions, preparing materials... All these little pieces require leadership to pull off. And with these practices in events that will not affect your professional career, after you get a good feel of what it is like, you can move on to taking on a leadership role in projects at school or work. And hopefully over time all these practices will add up and you will be a much more holistic leader.

Soft skills are a key part to being an effective leader as well. Apart from professional expertise at the work place. So i encourage you to be as proficient in your learning of people skills and mastering interpersonal communication as well as being fluent in all the intricacies and details of your job description.

If you require a higher level of leadership training, i would encourage you to sign up for a course that would put you in much more challenging situations where you will be put to the test. This may be the push that you need to get you on your path to be the leader that you always thought that you could be.

Personally, I have always been a leader, not of a team, but of my own path. That instead of following in the footsteps of someone, or taking orders from bosses, i like to take charge of what i do with my time. And how to manage my career in that fashion. As much as i would like to tell myself that i am an effective leader, more often that not, i can honestly say i wish i was better. I wish i was better at managing my time, at managing my finances, at managing my work, and I have to always upgrade my leadership skills to ensure that I am effective in what I do. That I do not waste precious time.

Your leadership goals might be different from mine. Maybe you have an aspiration to be a head of a company, or division, or to lead a group in charitable work, or to be a leader of a travel tour group. Being a leader comes in all forms and shapes, and your soft skills can definitely by transferable in all areas.

So i challenge you to take leadership seriously and to think of ways to improve your leadership skills by placing yourself in situations where you can fine tune every aspect

The Merry Lady

of your personality when dealing with others. At the end of the day, how people perceive you may be the most important factor of all.

I hope you learned something today, take care and as always, i will see you in the next one.

The Merry Lady

PART 2

Chapter 1:
Achieving Happiness

Happiness is a topic that is at the core of this channel. Because as humans we all want to be happy in some way shape or form. Happiness strikes as something that we all want to strive for because how can we imagine living an unhappy life. It might be possible but it wouldn't be all that fun no matter how you spin it. However I'm gonna offer another perspective that would challenge the notion of happiness and one that maybe would be more attainable for the vast majority of people.

So why do we as humans search for happiness? It is partly due to the fact that it has been ingrained in us since young that we all should strive to live a happy and healthy life. Happiness has become synonymous with the very nature of existence that when we find ourselves unhappy in any given moment, we tend to want to pivot our life and the current situation we are in to one that is more favourable, one that is supposedly able to bring us more happiness.

But how many of us are actually always happy all the time? I would argue that happiness is not at all sustainable if we were feeling it at full blast constantly. After a while we would find ourselves being numb to it and maybe that happiness would turn into neutrality or even boredom. There were times in my life where i felt truly happy and free. I felt that i had great friends around me, life had limitless possibilities, the weather was great, the housing situation was great, and i never wanted it to end as i knew that it was the best time of my life.

However knowing that this circumstance is only temporary allowed me to cherish each and every moment more meaningfully. As i was aware that time was not infinite and that some day this very state of happiness would somehow end one way or another, that i would use that time wisely and spend them with purpose and meaning. And it was

The Merry Lady

this sense that nothing ever lasts forever that helped me gain a new perspective on everything i was doing at that present moment in time. Of course, those happy times were also filled with times of trials, conflicts, and challenges, and they made that period of my life all the more memorable and noteworthy.

For me, happiness is a temporary state that does not last forever. We might be happy today but sad tomorrow, but that is perfectly okay and totally fine. Being happy all the time is not realistic no matter how you spin it. The excitement of getting a new house and new car would soon fade from the moment you start driving in it, and that happiness you once thought you associated with it can disappear very quickly. And that is okay. Because life is about constant change and nothing really ever stays the same.

With happiness comes with it a whole host of different emotions that aims to highlight and enhance its feeling. Without sadness and sorrow, happiness would have no counter to be matched against. It is like a yin without a yang. And we need both in order to survive.

I believe that to be truly happy, one has to accept that sadness and feelings of unhappiness will come as a package deal. That whilst we want to be happy, we must also want to feel periods of lull to make the experience more rewarding.

I challenge all of you today to view happiness as not something that is static and that once you achieved it that all will be well and life will be good, but rather a temporary state of feeling that will come again and again when you take steps to seek it.

I also want to bring forth to you an alternative notion to happiness, in the form of contentment, that we will discuss in the next video. Take care and I'll see you there.

Chapter 2:

The Only Obstacle Is Yourself

Ever wondered why you feel low all the time?

Why it seems like everyone is better than you?

Why everyone excels at something that you wished you were good at too?

I am sure you have wondered about at least one of these at one or another instance in your life.

These questions remain unanswered no matter how hard you try. Until you realize that the only answer that fits the puzzle is that, it is because of you.

All these barriers and limitations are placed upon you not because you are stupid or incapable.

It is merely because you have limiting beliefs about yourself that stop you from achieving your fullest potential.

It is because you are not trying hard enough to make yourself stand apart from everyone else in the world.

If you lag at school, study hard.

If your lag at your job, socialize more.

If you are obese, break a sweat to lose all that fat.

If you lack some technical skill, learn till you beat the very best in that field.

Don't blame others for your failures.

Everyone else starts off with the same resources and expertise as you.

If others can succeed, Why can't you?

Who is stopping you from flying high in victory?

If no one else tells you, let me do the honors; it's you.

You are the biggest cause of everything that is happening in your life right now.

Nothing is good or bad unless you do or don't do something to generate that result.

Make a promise to yourself today that you will achieve something great by the end of this week.

Envision the big picture and start watching yourself get drawn into that picture.

The Merry Lady

Take baby steps. take a big leap of faith.

Move one foot forward over the other no matter how big or small.

Once you get past the fear of being stuck where you currently are,

life will start opening great doors to your every step forward.

Sometimes we may take a step back.

Sometimes life throws us durians instead of lemons.

As long as you dust yourself off and move again you are never going to lose.

Don't idealize someone if you are not ready to idealize yourself.

To envision yourself charting your own path, in your own unique pair of shoes.

If for whatever reason you don't achieve that something someday, don't beat yourself up for it.

Maybe those shoes weren't the right fit for you.

Try another pair of shoes, and walk down a new path with confidence.

This could be a blessing in disguise for you.

A lesson for you to strive towards something new.

The Merry Lady

Something better. Something that no one has ever dreamed of or done before.

If along the way some someone comes and tells you to stop, and you stop to hear them say that to you, it wasn't their fault, but yours. Because you were idle enough to be distracted by others to compromise that dream.

Don't lift your head until you have achieved something today. Don't say a word to anyone about your goals.

Spend more and more time to figure out your life. Promise yourself that no one else matters in your life till you have achieved everything and you are left with nothing more to achieve.

I remember the time my father told me to be a better man than him. The time when I fell off my bicycle for the first time. He came to me and said, 'Don't give up now, as you will fall every day, but when you rise you will achieve bigger and better things than you could ever wish'.

My father gave me his hand when I needed it the most and he still does. But when he is gone and there is no one free enough or caring enough left to see me go through all that struggle, then I will be the closest figure to my father to back me up and give me the courage to get up and start again till I succeed in riding the bike of life.

You and I are capable of riding the high tide. Either we ride it all the way to the shore or we drown to never get back up again. It's up to us now what we want to do. It's you who decides what you were and what you can be!

You will regret yourself the most when you finally come to realize that it was 'You' who brought you down. So don't waste yourself and make a vow today, a vow to be the best you can be and the rest will be history.

Chapter 3:
Fight Lethargy and Win

Life is a continuous grind. Life is the summation of our efforts. Life is series of things that no one thinks can happen. But they do, and they do for a reason. Your life is no different than anyone else. You have the same needs and somewhat the same goals. But you might still be a failure while the world moves on. Let me explain why.

People always misunderstand having a humble mindset as opposed to having a go-getter mindset. The difference between you and a successful person is the difference in mindset.

When you think that you are not feeling well today to go to the gym. That you are not motivated enough to do some cardio or run that treadmill. That you didn't have a good day and now you are feeling down so you should stay in bed because you think you deserve some time off. This is the moment you messed up your life.

What you should have done is to tell yourself, What have I achieved today that made me deserving of this time off. You didn't!

How can you sit back and remain depressed when no one else feels sorry for you but only you do. Because you still haven't come to realize that no one will give you sympathy for something you made a mess of. And you are still not willing enough to make things happen for yourself.

When you have nothing, you think someone owes you something. That someone handles something bad that happens in your life. The reality is far from this.

It is fine if you are going through some rough patch in your life right now. But don't try to put the blame on others and back off of your responsibilities and duties. You have something to move towards but you are still sitting there waiting for the moment to come to your doorstep. But it ain't gonna happen. It's never an option to wait!

Don't just sit there and make strategies and set goals. Get up and start acting on those plans. The next plan will come by default.

You shouldn't feel depressed about the bad things, you should feel anger for why did you let those things happen to you in the first place. What did you lag that made you come to this stage right now. Why were you so lazy enough to let those results slide by you when your gut told you to do something different. But you didn't. And now it has all come to haunt you once again.

But you don't need that attitude. What you need is to stop analyzing and start doing something different rather than contemplate what you could have done.

The moments you lost will never come back, so there is no point in feeling sorry for those moments in this present moment. Use this moment to get the momentum you need.

Now is the time to prove yourself wrong, to make this life worth living for.

Now is the time to spend the most valuable asset of your life on something you want the most in your life. Now is the time to use all that energy and bring a change to your life that you will cherish for the rest of your life and in that afterlife.

Prove to yourself that you are worthy of that better life. That no one else deserves more than you. Because you made a cause for yourself. You ran all your life and struggled for that greater good.

Destiny carves its path when your show destiny what you have to offer.

The Merry Lady

You want to succeed in life, let me tell you the simplest way to that success; get up, go outside and get to work.

When you feel the lowest in your life, remember, you only start to lose that fat, when you start to sweat and you feel the heat and the pain coming through.

What you started yesterday, finish it today. Not tomorrow, not tonight, but right now!

Get working! It doesn't matter if it takes you an hour or 12 to complete the job. Do it. You will never fulfill the task if you keep thinking for the right moment. Every moment is the right moment.

You are always one decision away from a completely different life. You are always one moment away from the best moment of your life. But it is either this moment or it's never.

Chapter 4:
Twenty Percent of Effort Produces 80% of Results

Today we're going to talk about the 80-20 rule and how you can apply it to your life for great results in whatever you are doing. For the purposes of this video we are going to use income as a measurement of success. This will directly translate to productivity and the areas that you are spending your most time and energy.

Have you ever wondered why no matter how much time you end up working, that your paycheck never seems to rise? That your income and finance seems to be stagnant? Or have you ever wondered, for those of you who have ventured into creating a second or third stream of income on the side, that you might actually spend lesser on those activities and earn a bigger income in proportion to the time you actually spent to run those side businesses?

This is where the 80-20 rule comes into play. For those that have not seen their bank account or income grow despite the immense amount of effort put it, It may be that 80% of time you are spending it doing things that actually have little or no change to the growth of your networth. The work simply isn't actually worth 80% of your attention.

Rather you may want to look elsewhere, to that 20%, if you want to see real change. I would recommend that instead of banging your head against the wall at your day job, try looking for something to do on the side. It may be just your passion, or it may be something you foresee greater potential returns. Start taking action on those things. It could be the very thing that you were searching for this whole time. If the rule applies, you should be spending majority of your time and energy into this 20%. By focusing on the tasks that has the greatest rewards, you are working smart instead of working hard now. Only when you can identify what exactly those tasks are can you double down on them for great success.

There were times in my life that I spent a lot of my time trying to force something to work. But no matter how hard I tried, I just couldn't see a breakthrough. It was only after further exploration through trials and errors did I finally come up with a set list of tasks that I knew were profitable. That if I kept doing them over and over again I would be able to grow my wealth consistently. By spending all of my time doing these specific tasks, I was able to eliminate all the noise and to focus my actions to a narrow few. And I was surprised at the outsized rewards it brought me.

If you know that something isn't working, don't be afraid to keep looking, trying, and exploring other ways. Keep a close tab on the time you spend in these areas and the income that flows in. Only when you measure everything can you really know where you are going wrong and where you are going right.

Remember that 20% of the effort produces 80% of the results. So I challenge all of you to stop spending 80% of the effort doing things that only produce 20% of the results. It is better to work smart than to work hard. Trust me. I believe that you will be able to find what those things are if you put your mind to it.

I hope you learned something today, take care and I'll see you in the next one.

Chapter 5:
Happy People Choose to Exercise

There is a feeling you get when you just finish your workout, and you feel amazing, much better than you were feeling before. Even when you are not feeling motivated to go to the gym, just thinking about this feeling makes you get up, leave your bed and get going to the gym. This feeling can also be called an endorphin rush. Exercise indeed makes you happier in multiple ways.

Firstly, movement helps you bond with others that are in the brain chemistry of it all. Your heart rate is going up, you are using your body, engaging your muscles, your brain chemistry will change, and it will make it easier for you to connect and bond with other people. It also changes how your trust people. Research also showed that social pressures like a hug, laughing, or high-five are also enhanced. You will also find your new fitness fam, the people you will be working out with, and because you will have a shared interest that is having a healthy lifestyle will help you have a stronger bond with them. And as experts say that having strong relationships and connections in life will help you in overall happiness.

We have already discussed those exercise increases endorphins but what you do not know is that it increases a lot more brain chemicals that make you feel happy and good about yourself. Some of the brain chemicals that increase are; dopamine, endorphins, endocannabinoid and adrenaline. All of these chemicals are associated with feeling confident, capable, and happy. The amount of stress, physical pain, and anxiety also decrease significantly. A chemical that your body creates when your muscles contract is called "myokine", it is also shown to boost happiness and relieve stress.

Secondly, exercise can help boost your confidence, and of course, when it comes to feeling empowered and happy, confidence is the key. "At the point when you move with others, it's anything but a solid feeling of 'greater than self' probability that causes individuals to feel more idealistic and enabled, "Also, it permits individuals to feel more engaged turning around the difficulties in their own lives. What's more, that is a fascinating side advantage of moving with others because there's an encapsulated feeling of 'we're in the same boat' that converts into self-assurance and the capacity to take on difficulties in your day; to day existence."

Thirdly, exercising outdoors affects your brain, similar to meditation. In case you're similar to the innumerable other people who have found out about the advantages of contemplation yet can't make the time, uplifting news. You may not need to contemplate to get a portion of the advantages. Researchers found that exercising outside can similarly affect the cerebrum and disposition as reflection. Exercising outside immediately affects a state of mind that is amazingly incredible for wretchedness and nervousness. Since it's anything but a state in your mind that is the same as contemplation, the condition of open mindfulness,"

Chapter 6:
8 Ways To Love Yourself First

"Your task is not to seek for love, but merely to seek and find all the barriers within yourself that you have built against it." - Rumi.

Most of us are so busy waiting for someone to come into our lives and love us that we have forgotten about the one person we need to love the most – ourselves. Most psychologists agree that being loved and being able to love is crucial to our happiness. As quoted by Sigmund Freud, "love and work … work and love. That's all there is." It is the mere relationship of us with ourselves that sets the foundation for all other relationships and reveals if we will have a healthy relationship or a toxic one.

Here are some tips on loving yourself first before searching for any kind of love in your life.

1. Know That Self-Love Is Beautiful

Don't ever consider self-love as being narcissistic or selfish, and these are two completely different things. Self-love is rather having positive regard for our wellbeing and happiness. When we adopt self-love, we see higher levels of self-esteem within ourselves, are less critical and harsh with ourselves while making mistakes, and can celebrate our positive qualities and accept all our negative ones.

2. Always be kind to yourself:

We are humans, and humans are tended to get subjected to hurts, shortcomings, and emotional pain. Even if our family, friends, or even our partners may berate us about our inadequacies, we must learn to accept ourselves with all our imperfections and flaws. We look for acceptance from others and be harsh on ourselves if they tend to be cruel or heartless with us. We should always focus on our many positive qualities, strengths, and abilities, and admirable traits; rather than harsh judgments, comparisons, and self-hatred get to us. Always be gentle with yourself.

3. Be the love you feel within yourself:

You may experience both self-love and self-hatred over time. But it would be best if you always tried to focus on self-love more. Try loving yourself and having positive affirmations. Do a love-kindness meditation or spiritual practices to nourish your soul, and it will help you feel love and compassion toward yourself. Try to be in that place of love throughout your day and infuse this love with whatever interaction you have with others.

4. Give yourself a break:

We don't constantly live in a good phase. No one is perfect, including ourselves. It's okay to not be at the top of your game every day, or be happy all the time, or love yourself always, or live without pain. Excuse your bad days and embrace all your imperfections and mistakes. Accept your negative emotions but don't let them overwhelm you. Don't set high standards for yourself, both emotionally and mentally. Don't judge yourself for whatever you feel, and always embrace your emotions wholeheartedly.

5. Embrace yourself:

Are you content to sit all alone because the feelings of anxiety, fear, guilt, or judgment will overwhelm you? Then you have to practice being comfortable in your skin. Go within and seek solace in yourself, practice moments of alone time and observe how you treat yourself. Allow yourself to be mindful of your beliefs, feelings, and thoughts, and embrace solitude. The process of loving yourself starts with understanding your true nature.

6. Be grateful:

Rhonda Bryne, the author of The Magic, advises, "When you are grateful for the things you have, no matter how small they may be, you will see those things instantly increase." Look around you and see all the things that you are blessed to have. Practice gratitude daily and be thankful for all the things, no matter how good or bad they are. You will immediately start loving yourself once you realize how much you have to be grateful for.

7. Be helpful to those around you:

You open the door for divine love the moment you decide to be kind and compassionate toward others. "I slept and dreamt that life was a joy. I awoke and saw that life was service. I acted, and behold, and service was a joy." - Rabindranath Tagore. The love and positive vibes that you wish upon others and send out to others will always find a way back to you. Your soul tends to rejoice when you are kind, considerate, and compassionate. You have achieved the highest form of self-love when you decide to serve others. By helping others, you will realize that you don't need someone else to feel complete; you are complete. It will help you feel more love and fulfillment in your life.

8. Do things you enjoy doing:

If you find yourself stuck in a monotonous loop, try to get some time out for yourself and do the things that you love. There must be a lot of hobbies and passions that you might have put a brake on. Dust them off and start doing them again. Whether it's playing any sport, learning a new skill, reading a new book, writing in on your journal, or simply cooking or baking for yourself, start doing it again. We shouldn't compromise on the things that make us feel alive. Doing the things we enjoy always makes us feel better about ourselves and boost our confidence.

Conclusion:

Loving yourself is nothing short of a challenge. It is crucial for your emotional health and ability to reach your best potential. But the good news is, we all have it within us to believe in ourselves and live the best life we possibly can. Find what you are passionate about, appreciate yourself, and be grateful for what's in your life. Accept yourself as it is.

Chapter 7:

Happy People Spend Time Alone

No man is an island except for similarly as we blossom with human contact and connections, so too would we be able to prosper from time burned through alone. Also, this, maybe, turns out to be particularly important right now since we're all in detachment. We've since quite a while ago slandered the individuals who decide to be distant from everyone else, except isolation shouldn't be mistaken for forlornness. Here are two mental reasons why investing energy in isolation makes us more joyful and more satisfied:

1. Spending time alone reconnects us.

Our inclination for isolation might be transformative, as indicated by an examination distributed in the British Journal of Psychology in 2016. Utilizing what they call "the Savannah hypothesis of satisfaction," transformative clinicians Satoshi Kanazawa of the London School of Economics and Norman Li of Singapore Management University accept that the single, tracker accumulate way of life of our precursors structure the establishment of what satisfies us in present-day times. The group examined a study of 15,000 individuals matured somewhere between 18 and 28 in the United States. They found that individuals living in more thickly populated regions were fundamentally less cheerful than the individuals who lived in more modest networks.

"The higher the populace thickness of the prompt climate, the less glad" respondents were. The scientists accept this is because we had advanced mentally from when mankind, for the most part, existed on distant, open savannahs. Since quite a while ago, we have instilled an inclination to be content alone, albeit current life generally neutralizes that. Also, as good to beat all, they tracked down that the more clever an individual was, the more they appreciated investing energy alone. Along these lines, isolation makes you more joyful AND is evidence of your smarts. We're in.

2. Spending Time Alone Teaches Us Empathy

Investing in a specific measure of energy alone can create more compassion towards others than a milestone concentrate from Harvard. Scientists found that when enormous gatherings of individuals encircle us, it's harder for us to acquire viewpoints and tune into the sensations of others. However, when we venture outside that unique circumstance, the extra headspace implies we can feel for the situation of individuals around us in a more genuine and significant manner. Furthermore, that is uplifting news for others, but different investigations show that compassion and helping other people are significant to prosperity and individual satisfaction.

"At the point when you invest energy with a specific friend network or your colleagues, you foster a 'we versus them' attitude," clarifies psychotherapist and creator Amy Morin. "Investing energy alone assists you with growing more empathy for individuals who may not find a way into your 'inward circle.' "On the off chance that you're not used to isolation, it can feel awkward from the outset," she adds. "However, making that tranquil time for yourself could be critical to turning into the best form of yourself."

Chapter 8:

Overcome Demotivation

Human life is very short and keeps getting shorter and shorter with each day. In this short life we feel discouraged and every other moment or every other day. We get frustrated and we tend to lose hope.

But then good days come too and we feel on top of the world. Our hearts are overfilled with joy and satisfaction but this too lasts for some time and then life surprises us with some new big rock of grief or depression. This moment though short can take us down a deep hole where we don't see a way back up.

This is the moment of everyone's life where they are the most demotivated to do anything in life. No matter how much our loved ones try to get us to try one more time, we keep sinking deeper into self-rejection and denial.

This feeling of not being motivated no matter what good comes around time after time is not helpful for anyone even if you need to become the world's most successful person.

But there are countless things you can do to deviate your mind from any such situation. Let's discuss some.

I'll say, you get up right away, tighten up some shoes and get out on a long run. Try to look around you and find anyone else who can apparently be in any distress. Approach them if you can and help them in any way possible if they allow you to.

Try to feel others' pain and surely you will be thankful for what you already have in life.

If you don't feel like going out that's OK too; pick up the phone and call anyone who you think might care for the most for what you are going through right now. If you have someone who can relate to you in such times of greys and blacks, you surely have an escape route.

You might think you are sitting alone on your couch in your sweats and wandering over random things to take your mind off.

But the reality is that every now and then in such alone moments you wander off in conditions where you somehow end up comparing yourself with someone else and rather than being inspired by that person, you feel jealous and might curse someone. You start to think what they have is perfect and you can never be there. But the reality is they are there because they knew how to overcome these feelings you have right now.

So reorder yourself. Make a new plan. Make a new scheme for what you should be doing when the next fire breaks in your life. What you can do to overcome the next rejection.

Things have always a way to release you. Events can leave an impact but that impact doesn't necessarily have to stamp rather a lesson to take new paths. You don't want to put your hands in the same hole again where you were once bitten. You just need to find a way to get around the hole and keep the track you were once on!

Chapter 9:
Happy People Surround Themselves with The Right People

Whether we realized it or not, we become like the five people we spend the most time with. We start behaving like them, thinking like them, looking like them. We even make decisions based on what we think they would want us to do.

For example, there are many research findings that prove we are more likely to gain weight if a close friend or a family member becomes overweight. Similarly, we are more likely to engage in an exercise program if we surround ourselves with fit and health-oriented people.

So, who are the top 5 influencers in your life? Do they make you feel positive? Do they inspire and motivate you to be the best version of yourself? Do they support and encourage you to achieve your goals? Or, do they tell you that "it can't be done," "it's not possible," "you aren't good enough," "you will most likely fail."

If you feel emotionally drained by the energetic vampires in your life, you may want to detox your life and get rid of the relationships that aren't serving you in a positive way.

The negative people, the naysayers, the Debbie Downers, and the chronic complainers are like a dark cloud over your limitless potential.

They hold you back and discourage you from even trying because they're afraid that if you succeed, you'll prove them wrong.

Have the courage to remove the negative people from your life and watch how your energy and enthusiasm automatically blossom. Letting go of the relationships that aren't serving us is a critical step if we want to become more positive, fulfilled, and successful.

Detoxing your life from negative influencers will also allow you to become the person you truly want to be. You'll free yourself from constant judgment, negativity, and lack of support.

Here's what you can do:

- Stay away from chronic complainers.
- Stop participating in meaningless conversations.
- Share your ideas only with people who are supportive or willing to provide constructive criticism.
- Minimize your interactions with "friends," coworkers, and family members who are negative, discouraging, and bitter.
- Stop watching TV and reading negative posts on social media (yes, mainstream media is a major negative influence in our lives!).
- Surround yourself with positive and successful people (remember, we become like the top 5 people we spend our time with!).

- Find new, like-minded friends, join networking and support groups, or find a positive coach or a mentor.

If you want to make a positive change in your life, remember, the people around you have a critical influence on your energy, growth, and probability of success.

Positive people bring out the best in you and make you feel motivated and happy. They help you when you're in need, encourage you to go after your dreams, and are there to celebrate your successes or support you as you move past your challenges. Pick your top 5 wisely!

Chapter 10:
Happy People Live Slow

"Slow Living means **structuring your life around meaning and fulfilment**. Similar to 'voluntary simplicity and 'downshifting,' it emphasizes a **less-is-more approach**, focusing on the quality of your life…Slow Living addresses the desire to lead a more balanced life and pursue a **more holistic sense of well-being** in the fullest sense of the word. In addition to the personal advantages, there are potential **environmental benefits** as well. When we slow down, we often use fewer resources and produce less waste, both of which have a lighter impact on the earth."

Slow living is a state of mind it will make you feel purposeful and is more fulfilling. It is all about being consistent and steady. Now that you have an idea of slow living, we will break down some myths attached to slow living and how to start slow living for mind peace and happiness. The first myth is that slow living is about doing everything as slowly as possible. Slow living is not about doing everything in slow motion but doing things at the right speed and not rushing. It is all about gaining time so you can do things that are important to you. The second myth is that slow living is the same as simple living. Now simple living is more worldly, and simple living is more focused on time.

The third myth is that slow living is an aesthetic that you see on desaturated Instagram posts, but that is not true; this is considered a minimalist aesthetic, whereas slow living is a minimalist lifestyle. The 4th myth is that slow living is about doing and being less. That is not at all true. It is all about removing the non-essentials from your life so you can have more time to be yourself. And the last myth is that slow living is anti-technology now. This is not about travelling back in time but all about using tech as a tool and not vice versa.

If you like this idea of living, we are going to list ten ways in which you can start slow living;

1. Define what is most important to you(essentials)
2. Say no to everything else (non-essentials)
3. Understand busyness and that it is a choice
4. Create space and margin in your day and life
5. Practice being present
6. Commit to putting your life before work
7. Adopt a slow information diet
8. Get outside physically and connect dots mentally
9. Start slow and small by downshifting
10. Find inspiration in the slow living community

Sit back and think about what the purpose of your life is, what you ultimately want from your life and not just in a monetary sense. Think about what you would like for your lifestyle to be 50 years from now, and then start working on it today. Suppose you have not figured out the purpose. In that case, there are multiple personality tests available on the internet that will help you determine your personality type and then eventually help you create your purpose.

PART 3

Chapter 1:
How To Worry Less

How many of you worry about little things that affect the way you go about your day? That when you're out with your friends having a good time or just carrying out your daily activities, when out of nowhere a sudden burst of sadness enters your heart and mind and immediately you start to think about the worries and troubles you are facing. It is like you're fighting to stay positive and just enjoy your day but your mind just won't let you. It becomes a tug of war or a battle to see who wins?

How many of you also lose sleep because your mind starts racing at bedtime and you're flooded with sad feelings of uncertainty, despair, worthlessness or other negative emotions that when you wake up, that feeling of dread immediately overwhelms you and you just feel like life is too difficult and you just dont want to get out of bed.

Well If you have felt those things or are feeling those things right now, I want to tell you you're not alone. Because I too struggle with those feelings or emotions on a regular basis.

At the time of writing this, I was faced with many uncertainties in life. My business had just ran into some problems, my stocks weren't doing well, I had lost money, my bank account was telling me I wasn't good enough, but most importantly, i had lost confidence. I had lost the ability to face each day with confidence that things will get better. I felt that i was worthless and that bad things will always happen to me. I kept seeing the negative side of things and it took a great deal of emotional toll on me. It wasn't like i chose to think and feel these things, but they just came into my mind whenever they liked. It was like a parasite feeding off my negative energy and thriving on it, and weakening me at the same time.

The Merry Lady

Now your struggles may be different. You may have a totally different set of circumstances and struggles that you're facing, but the underlying issue is the same. We all go through times of despair, worry, frustration, and uncertainty. And it's totally normal and we shouldn't feel ashamed of it but to accept that it is a part of life and part of our reality.

But there are things we can do to minimise these worries and to shift to a healthier thought pattern that increases our ability to fight off these negative emotions.

I want to give you 5 actionable steps that you can take to worry less and be happier. And these steps are interlinked that can be carried out in fluid succession for the greatest benefit to you. But of course you can choose whichever ones speaks the most to you and it is more important that you are able to practice any one of these steps consistently rather than doing all 5 of them haphazardly. But I want to make sure I give you all the tools so that you can make the best decisions for yourself.

Try this with me right now as I go through these 5 steps and experience the benefit for yourself instead of waiting until something bad happens.

The very first step is simple. Just breathe. When a terrible feeling of sadness rushes into your body out of nowhere, take that as a cue to close your eyes, stop whatever you are doing, and take 5 deep breathes through your nose. Breathing into your chest and diaphragm. Deep breathing has the physiological benefit of calming your nerves and releasing tension in the body and it is a quick way to block out your negative thoughts. Pause the video if you need to do practice your deep breathing before we move on.

And as you deep breathe, begin the second step. Which is to practice gratefulness. Be grateful for what you already have instead of what you think u need to have to be happy. You could be grateful for your dog, your family, your friends, and whatever means the most to you. And if you cannot think of anything to be grateful for, just be grateful that you are even alive and walking on this earth today because that is special and amazing in its own right.

Next is to practice love and kindness to yourself. You are too special and too important to be so cruel to yourself. You deserve to be loved and you owe it to yourself to be kind and forgiving. Life is tough as it is, don't make it harder. If you don't believe in yourself, I believe in you and I believe in your worthiness as a person that you have a lot left to give.

The fourth step is to Live Everyday as if it were your last. Ask yourself, will you still want to spend your time worrying about things out of your control if it was your last day on earth? Will you be able to forgive yourself if you spent 23 out of the last 24 hours of your life worrying? Or will you choose to make the most out of the day by doing things that are meaningful and to practice love to your family, friends, and yourself?

Finally, I just want you to believe in yourself and Have hope that whatever actions you are taking now will bear fruition in the future. That they will not be in vain. That at the end of the day, you have done everything to the very best of your ability and you will have no regrets and you have left no stone unturned.

How do you feel now? Do you feel that it has helped at least a little or even a lot in shaping how you view things now? That you can shift your perspective and focus on the positives instead of the worries?

If it has worked for you today, I want to challenge you to consistently practice as many of these 5 steps throughout your daily lives every single day. When you feel a deep sadness coming over you, come back to this video if you need guidance, or practice these steps if you remember them on your own.

I wish you only good things and I hope that I have helped you that much more today. Thank you for your supporting me and this channel and if you find that I can do more for you, do subscribe to my channel and I'll see you in the next one. Take care.

Chapter 2:
Happy People Do What Matters to Them

Think about what you want most out of life. What were you created for? What is your mission in life? What is your passion? You were put on this earth for a reason, and knowing that reason will help you determine your priorities.

I spent a total of four months in the hospital, healing from my sickness. During that time, I spent a lot of time thinking about my purpose in life. I discovered that my purpose is to help you change your lives by focusing on what matters most to you.

1. Create A Plan

Create a plan to get from where you are today to where you want to be. Maybe you need a new job. Maybe you need to go back to school. Maybe you need to deal with some relationship issues. Whatever it is, create a plan that will get you to where you want to be.

While I was in the hospital, I began to draft my life plan. My plan guides all of my actions, helps me focus on my relationships with my wife and daughter, and helps me keep working toward my life purpose. A life plan will help you focus your life too.

2. Focus On Now

Stop multitasking and focus on one thing at a time. It may be a project at work. It may be a conversation with your best friend. It may just be the book that you have wanted to read for months. The key is to focus on one thing at a time.

I plan each day the night before by picking the three most important tasks from my to-do list. In the morning, I focus on each one of these tasks individually until they are completed. Once I complete these three tasks, I check email, return phone calls, etc.

3. Just Say "No."

We all have too much to do and too little time. The only way you will find the time for the things that matter is to say "no" to the things that don't.

I use my purpose and life plan to make decisions about the projects and tasks I say yes to. If a project or task is not aligned with my purpose, a good fit with my life plan, and sometimes that I have time to accomplish, I say no to the project. Saying no to good opportunities gives you time to focus on the best opportunities.

Research tells us that 97 percent of people are living their life by default and not by design. They don't know where their life is headed and don't plan what they want to accomplish in life.

These steps will help you to decide what matters most to you. They will help you to begin living your life by design and not by default. Most importantly, they will help you to create a life focused on what matters to you.

Let me end by asking, "What matters most to you?

The Lure of Wanting Luxury Items

Have you ever walked by a store and pondered over those LV bags if you were a lady? Secretly hoping that you can get your hands on one of those bags so that you can feel good about yourself when you carry them on your shoulders? Or have you ever glanced at a boutique watch shop if you were a guy hoping that you can get your hands on one of the rolexes which costs north of $10k minimum? That could be the same lust and desire for the latest and greatest cars, apple products, clothing, etc. anything you name it.

You think of saving up a year's worth of salary just to be able to afford one of these things and you see yourself feeling good about it and that you can brag to your friends and show off to people that you have the latest and most expensive product on the market. and you imagine yourself being happy that it is all you will need to stay happy.

I am here to tell you that the lure of owning luxury items can only make you happy to a certain extent. And only if purchasing these things is something of great meaning to you, like achieving a big milestone that you want to commemorate in life. In that instance, walking into that store to purchase that luxury product can be a great experience and of great significance as well. Whether it be a birthday gift to yourself, or commemorating a wedding anniversary, job/career work milestone, or any of that in nature, you will tend to hold these products with great sentimental value and hardly will you ever sell these items should the opportunity arise to make a profit from them (which is generally not the case with most things you buy).

I will argue that when you pick these products to wear from your wardrobe, you will indeed be filled with feelings of happiness, but it is not the product itself that makes you happy, but it is the story behind it, the hard work, the commemorative occasion that you will associate and remember these products for. It will transport you back in time to that place in your life when you made the purchase and you will indeed relive that emotion that took you there to the store in the first place. That to me is a meaningful luxury purchase that is not based on lust or greed, but of great significance.

But what if you are just someone who is chasing these luxury products just because everyone else has it? When you walk down the street and you see all these people carrying these products and you just tell yourself you have to have it or else? You find all the money you can dig from your savings and emergency fund to pay for that product? I would argue that in that instance, you will not be as happy as you thought you would be. These kinds of wants just simply do not carry the weight of any importance. And after feeling good for a few days after you owned that luxury good, you feel a deep sense of emptiness because it really does not make you a happier person. Instead you are someone trying to have something but with that comes a big hole in your wallet or your bank account. The enthusiasm and excitement starts to fade away and you wonder whats the next luxury good you need to buy to feel that joy again.

You see, material goods cannot fill us with love and happiness. Luxury goods are only there to serve one purpose, to reward you for your hard work and that you can comfortably purchase it without regret and worry that you are left financially in trouble. The lure of many of us is that we tend to want what we can't have. It could also turn into an obsession for many of us where we just keep buying more and more of these luxury goods to satisfy our craving for materialistic things. You will realise one day that the pursuit never ends, the more you see, the more you want. And that is just how our brains are wired.

I have a confession to make, I had an obsession for apple products myself and I always thought I wanted the latest and greatest apple products every year when a new model comes out. And every year apple seems to know how to satisfy my lust for these products and manages to make me spend thousands of dollars every time they launch something new. This addiction i would say lasted for a good 8 years until I recently realised that the excitement ALWAYS fades after a week or two. Sure it is exciting to play with it for a couple of days while your brain gets used to this incredible piece of technology sitting in front of you. But after a week or two, I am left wondering, whats

The Merry Lady

next? I began to realise that what really made me happy was doing what i love, engaging in my favourite hobbies, meeting friends, and just living simply without so many wants in life. When you have less wants, you automatically go into a mindset of abundance. And that is a great feeling to have.

I challenge all of you today to question what is your real motivation behind wanted to buy luxury items. Is it to commemorate a significant achievement in your life? or is it a meaningless lust for something that you want to emulate others for. Dig deeper and you will find the answer. Thank you

Chapter 3:
Pressures of Social Media

Ah social media. This piece of technology has he power to either make us better people and more connected, or wreck us all completely. I want to address this topic today because I feel that social media is a tool that has uses that can impact us either negatively or positively, depending on how we use it. For the purpose of this video, we will talk about how social media can affect our self-worth and self-esteem.

For most of us, when we first hop onto social media, our goal is to connect with our friends. We hop onto Facebook and Instagram to add our friends and to see what's up in their lives, and to be involved with them digitally so to speak. We start by chatting them up and checking out their photos and posts. And we feel happy to be part of a bigger network.

However sooner or later, we get sucked into the pressure of acquiring more people to boost our profile... to get more likes... to get more followers... to become... famous. And every time we post something, we always feel inferior that we don't have as many likes as our friends. That we are somehow unpopular. Furthermore, we start comparing our lives with our friends, and we see what a wonderful life they have lived, the amazing photos that they have taken around the world, and we start wondering where we had gone wrong in our lives, and why we are in such a "terrible" state. We start to wonder if we had made a mistake in our career paths and we constantly compare ourselves to others that make ourselves feel Low.

Another pressure we face from social media is in the area of body image and self-worth. We see posts of the world of the insta-famous, their chiseled bodies, their chiseled faces, their amazing hair, amazingly toned skin and beauty standards that we just can't help but compare ourselves to. We start feeling inferior and we start to think we are not beautiful. We then look for ways to improve the way we look that always makes us feel so lousy about ourselves. What's more is that we come across posts of people with amazing houses and with money beyond our wildest imaginations and we again beat ourselves up for it. We wonder why we are not in that same place in life as them.

Every time we open the app to see these accounts, this regular and constant comparisons leaves us with terrible Low self-esteem and self-worth that manifests in us day in and day out. And over time, it becomes part of our negative outlook on our own lives.

I had subjected myself to a few of these before when I first started out on social media. It became all too easy to bow to the pressure of social media when all you are feeding your mind every single day is the same exactly self-harming thing.

It was only after I took a break from social media and had time to grow up a little bit that I started to use social media in a much healthier way.

After coming back to social media after a long hiatus, I stopped chasing likes, stop chasing new followers, and focused on merely reconnecting once again with my friends. I stopped browsing random accounts that will always get me lost in this rabbit hole and I felt much better about myself. As I grew up, I stopped comparing myself to others but rather view people who are in better places than I was as ways to inspire me. I started to fill my accounts with people that would inspire me to get me where I want to be whether it be financially or physically. This profound shift in the way I used social media actually got me fired up each day to work towards my goals.

Using social media as a tool of inspiration, I found myself excited to start making more money from each of my followers' inspirational posts. Whether it be from following tony-Robbins, accounts created by warren buffet followers, to people who were successful in YouTube and other online business platforms, I was motivated every time I logged in rather than leaving feeling worthless.

Who you follow matters and how you choose to use social media matters as well. If you choose comparison rather than inspiration, you will always feel like you are unworthy. If you view other's success as a motivator, you can choose to follow people that inspire you each and every day to get you where you want to go.

I challenge each and every one of you to align your goals with social media. Think hard about what you want to use it for. Is it a means of escape? Or is it a tool for you to get cracking on your goals. If you wish to be healthier, follow people who inspire you each day to start working out rather than those that posts photos that only serve to show off their physique. If you want to be richer, following successful people who teach you life principles to be wealthy, rather than accounts that merely show off their incredible wealth with things they buy and the branded stuff they own. If you goal is to be a better person, there are plenty of accounts that seek to inspire. Maybe Oprah Winfrey would be a good person to o follow, if she has an account.

Choose who you follow wisely because their daily posts will have a direct consequences to how you start seeing things around you.

Chapter 4:

Do You Know What You Want?

Do you know who you are? Do you know what you are? Do you know what you want to become? Do you have any idea what you might become?

Every sane human has asked these questions to themselves multiple times in their lives. We have a specific trait of always finding the right answers to everything. We humans always try to find the meaning behind everything.

It's in our built-in nature to question everything around us. Yet we are here in this modern era of technology and resources and we don't have a sense of purpose. We don't have a true set of goals. We don't give enough importance to our future to take a second and make a long-term plan for longer gains.

The fault in our thinking is that we don't have a strict model of attention. We have too many distractions in our lives to spare a moment to clear our minds.

The other thing that makes us confused or ignorant is the fact that people have a way of leading us into thinking things that are not ours to start with.

Society has made these norms that have absolutely nothing to do with anyone except that these were someone's experience when they were once at our stage. We are dictated on things that are not ours to achieve but only a mere image of what others want us to achieve or don't.

No one has the right to tell you anything. No one has a right to say anything to you except if they are advising or reminding you of the worst. But to inflict a scenario with such surety that it will eventually happen to you because you have a fault that many others had before you is the most superstitious and illogical thing to do on any planet let alone Earth.

No one knows what the future holds for anyone. No one can guarantee even the next breath that they take. So why put yourself under someone else's spell of disappointment? Why do you feel the need to satisfy every person's whim? Why do you feel content with everyone around you getting their ways?

You always know in your heart, deep down in some corner what you want. You will always know what you need to be fulfilled. You will always find an inspiration within yourself to go and pursue that thing. What you need are some self-confidence and some self-motivation. You need to give yourself some time to straighten up your thoughts and you will eventually get the BOLD statement stating 'This is what I want'.

You don't need to shut everyone around you. You just need to fix your priorities and you will get a vivid image of what things are and what they can become.

There is no constraint of age or gender to achieving anything. These are just mental and emotional hurdles that we have imposed on our whole race throughout our history.

Just remember. When you know what you want, and you want it bad enough to give away everything for that, you will someday find a way to finally get it.

The Merry Lady

Chapter 5:

7 Ways On How To Attract Success In Life

Successful people fail more times than unsuccessful people try. A new thought author and metaphysical writer Florence Scovel Shinn in her timeless 1940 novel, 'the secret door to success,' suggests that "Success is not a secret, it is a system." Throughout the centuries, the leaders have alluded to the possibility that success can be attracted into one's life simply by thinking and doing. It is rather a planned journey as we give validity to the premise of creating a plan or setting a goal for ourselves. Goals are set to be achieved, and achievements pave the way for success. Here are 7 Ways To Attract Success In Your Life:

1. Define What Success Means To You

Success is subjective to the person who seeks to obtain it, and the ideas may be different for each other. For some of us, success means wealth. For some, it means health and happiness. While for some, it is the mere effort of getting out of bed every day. But the thing that is most highlighted is that we can never get success without struggling. Every one of us wants success, but we do not know how to bring about that life-changing phenomenon that will take us to the zenith of our potential.

2. Begin with Gratitude:

92

From flying to the sky to crashing to the ground, be always thankful to wherever life takes you. Always start by being grateful for what you already have. Whether it's good or bad, we cannot climb the stairs of success without having experiences. If we make mistakes, we should make sure not to give up, rather learn from those mistakes. We must strive to embrace our flaws and imperfections. If we tend to fall seven times, we must have the energy to get up eight times. Whatever life throws us at, no matter the obstacles and challenges, we should always be in a state of gratitude and always be thankful for our learning.

3. Stop making excuses:

Your decisions lead to your destiny. If you are thinking about delaying your work or 'chilling' first, then someone else will take that opportunity for himself. You either grab on the opportunities from both hands, or you sit on the sidelines and watch someone else steal your spotlight. There's no concept of resting and being lazy when you have to work towards your goals and achieve your dreams. One of the major mistakes of unsuccessful people is that they make endless excuses. They would avoid their tasks in any way instead of working on them and actually doing them. You will attract success only if you put your mind towards something and work hard towards it.

4. Realize your potential:

The fine line between incredibly hardworking people and yet fail to achieve success, and the ones who are at the peak of their respective field is simple – potential. We never realize our true potential until we are put in a situation where there's no way out but to express our abilities. We might think that people have more excellent skills than us or have more knowledge than us. But the truth is, we have more potential inside of us. This might be tougher to implement as we don't know how well we can handle things while stressing out or how much hidden talents and skills we possess. Our potential is merely what might make us successful or a failure. It all depends on how much we are willing to try and push ourselves forward.

5. Celebrate the success of others:

What you wish upon others finds its way and comes back to you again. While seeing people being successful in their professional and personal lives and making a fortune in their careers and businesses can be tough on our lives, always remember that they too faced struggles and challenges before reaching here. There's no need to be envious as life has an abundance of everything to offer to everyone. Whatever is it in your destiny will always find its way to you. You can't snatch what others have achieved, and similarly, others can't seize whatever that you have or may achieve. Congratulate people around you and be excited for them. Send out positive vibes to everyone so you may receive the same.

6. Behave as if you are successful:

Have you heard of the term "fake it till you make it?" Well, it applies to this scenario too. You can fake your success and act like a successful person until you really become one. First, surround yourself with lucrative people. See what habits they have developed over time, how they dress up, how they behave, and, most importantly, how much work they do daily to achieve their goals. Get inspired from them and adopt their healthy habits. Be successful in your own eyes first so that eventually you can be successful in other's eyes as well.

7. Provide value for others:

While money and fame are the most common success goals, we should first try to focus on creating value in the world. A lot of successful people wanted to change things in the world first and help people out. Mark Zuckerberg built a tool for Harvard students initially and now has over 1.4 billion users. The first thing on our mind after waking up shouldn't be money or success, and it would be to create value for the world and the people around us.

Conclusion:

It would be best if you strived to explore the unique, endless possibilities within you. Then, when you start working on yourself, you're adding to your mind's youth, vitality, and beauty.

Chapter 6:
6 Steps To Focus On Growth

Growth is a lifelong process. We grow every moment from the day we are born until our eventual death. And the amazing thing about growth is that there is no real limit to it.

Now, what exactly is growth? Well, growing is the process of changing from one state to another and usually, it has to be positive; constructive; better-than-before. Although growth occurs equally towards all directions in the early years of our life, the rate of growth becomes more and more narrowed down to only a few particular aspects of our life as we become old. We become more distinctified as individuals, and due to our individuality, not everyone of us can possibly grow in all directions. With our individual personality, experiences, characteristics, our areas of growth become unique to us. Consequently, our chances of becoming successful in life corresponds to how we identify our areas of growth and beam them on to our activities with precision. Let us explore some ways to identify our key areas of growth and utilize them for the better of our life.

1. Identify Where You Can Grow

For a human being, growth is relative. One person cannot grow in every possible way because that's how humans are—we simply cannot do every thing at once. One person may grow in one way while another may grow in a completely different way. Areas of growth can be so unlike that one's positive growth might even seem like negative growth to another person's perspective. So, it is essential that we identify the prime areas where we need to grow. This can be done through taking surveys, asking people or critically analyzing oneself. Find out what lackings do you have as a human being, find out what others think that you lack as a human being. Do different things and note down where you are weak but you have to do it anyway. Then, make a list of those areas where you need growing and move on to the next step.

2. Accept That You Need To Grow In Certain Areas

After carefully identifying your lackings, accept these in your conscious and subconscious mind. Repeatedly admit to yourself and others that you lack so and so qualities where you wish to grow with time.

Never feel ashamed of your shortcomings. Embrace them comfortably because you cannot trully change yourself without accepting that you need to change. Growth is a dynamic change that drags you way out of your comfort zone and pushes you into the wild. And to start on this endeavor for growth, you need to have courage. Growth is a choice that requires acceptance and humility.

3. Remind Yourself of Your Shortcomings

You can either write it down and stick it on your fridge or just talk about it in front of people you've just met—this way, you'll constantly keep reminding yourself that you have to grow out of your lackings. And this remembrance will tell you to try—try improving little by little. Try growing.

It is important to remain consciously aware of these at all times because you never know when you might have to face what. All the little and big things you encounter every day are all opportunities of growth. This takes us to the fourth step:

4. Face Your Problems

Whatever you encounter, in any moment or place in your life is an opportunity created: an opportunity for learning. A very old adage goes: "the more we learn, the more we grow". So, if you don't face your problems and run away from them, then you are just losing the opportunity to learn from it, and thus, losing the opportunity of growing from it. Therefore, facing whatever life throws at you also has an important implication on your overall growth. Try to make yourself useful against all odds. Even if you fail at it, you will grow anyway.

5. Cross The Boundary

So, by now you have successfully identified your areas of growth, you have accepted them, you constantly try to remind yourself of them and you face everything that comes up, head on—never running away. You are already making progress. Now comes the step where you push yourself beyond your current status. You go out of what you are already facing and make yourself appear before even more unsettling circumstances.

This is a very difficult process, but if you grow out of here, nothing can stop you ever. And only a few people successfully make it through. You create your own problems, no one might support you and yet still, you try to push forward, make yourself overcome new heights of difficulties and grow like the tallest tree in the forest. You stand out of the crowd. This can only be done in one or two subjects in a lifetime. So make sure that you know where you want to grow. Where you want to invest that much effort, and time, and dedication. Then, give everything to it. Growth is a life's journey.

6. Embrace Your Growth

After you have crossed the boundary, there is no turning back. You have achieved new heights in your life, beyond what you thought you could have ever done. The area—the subject in which you tried to develop yourself, you have made yourself uniquely specialized in that particular area. You have outgrown the others in that field. It is time for you to make yourself habituated with that and embrace it gracefully. The wisdom you've accumulated through growth is invaluable—it has its roots deeply penetrated into your life. The journey that you've gone through while pursuing your growth will now define you. It is who you are.

As I've mentioned in the first line, "growth is a lifelong process". Growth is not a walk in the park, It is you tracking through rough terrains—steep heights and unexplored depths for an entire lifetime. Follow these simple yet difficult steps; grow into the tallest tree and your life will shine upon you like the graceful summer sun.

Chapter 7:

6 Tricks To Become More Aware Of Your Strengths

"Strength and growth come only through continuous effort and struggle." - Napoleon Hill.

While it is true that we tend to focus more on our weaknesses than on our strengths, it is also true that we should polish our strengths more than our weaknesses. This in no way means that we should consider ourselves superior to others and start looking away from that we have flaws. Unfortunately, most of us don't spend much time on self-reflection and self-awareness. But they are the vital aspects if we are thinking of improving ourselves in any way.

Here are 6 Tricks to become more aware of your strengths:

1. Decide to be more self-aware

Human beings are complicated creatures. Our minds are designed so that we tend to absorb more negative than positive thoughts about ourselves and others. For this reason, self-awareness is perhaps the most crucial thing in an individual's life. Self-awareness is the ability to look deep inside of yourself and monitor your emotions and reactions. It is the ability to allow yourself to be aware of your strengths, weaknesses, as well as your triggers, motivators, and other characteristics. We'll help you find a set of tricks and techniques that you can apply to polish your strengths in a self-awareness way; and how to use your strengths in a promising way.

2. Meditation:

The first thought that will come to your mind would be, "Is this person crazy? How can meditation help us improve our strengths?" But hear me out. The fresh breeze of the morning when everything is at peace, and you sit there inhaling all the good energy in and the bad energy out, your mind and thoughts would automatically become slow-paced and calm. Once you get to relax with yourself, you can analyze the things that have been happening in your life and develop possible solutions on how you can deal with them using your strengths. The positive energy and calming mood you will get after meditating would help you make your decisions wisely when you are under pressure and your mind is in chaos.

3. Labelling your thoughts:

More often, our thoughts reflect on our behavior and what makes us fail or succeed in life. People can genuinely relate to a situation where they could have possibly thought about a worst-case scenario, but in the end, nothing as such happened. Our anxiety and hopelessness don't come from the situation we are struggling with, but rather our thoughts make us believe in the worst possible things that could happen to us. But we're stronger than we give ourselves credit for. We have the power to control our negative thoughts and turn them into positive ones. We can list all the ideas and thinking that provide us with stress and tension and then label them as either useful or useless. If the particular thought is causing a significant effect in your life, you can work towards it to make your life better and less anxious. Know your priorities and take help from your strengths to tackle the problems.

4. Befriending your fears:

There's not a single person on this planet who isn't afraid of something. Be it the fear of losing your loved ones or any phobias of either animal, insects, heights, closed spaces, etc. There are also so many fears related to our self-worth and whether we are good enough, skilled enough, or deserving enough of anything. To accept these fears and work towards overcoming them is perhaps the most powerful thing one could do. It takes so much of a person's strength and willpower to befriend fear, reduce it, and finally eliminate it. Most of the time, we end up in situations that we always feared, and then we have to take quick actions and make wise decisions. To remain calm in such cases and use your strengths and experiences to tackle whatever's in front of you is a remarkable quality found in only a few. But we can also achieve and polish this quality by strengthening our minds and preparing ourselves to get us out of situations wisely and effectively. To be patient and look into the problems from every angle is the critical component of this one.

5. Watching your own movie:

Narrating your life experiences to yourself or a close friend and telling yourself and them how far you have come can boost your self-confidence immensely. You should go in flashbacks and try to remember all the details of your life. You will find that there were some moments you felt immense joy and some moments where you felt like giving up. But with all the strength that you were collecting along the way, you endured the possible tortures and struggles and challenges and eventually rose again. So you should focus and be well aware of how you tackle those situations, what powers you have, and the strengths that couldn't let you give up but face everything. Once you have found the answers to the above questions, like for example, it was your patience and bravery that helped you through it, or it was your wise and speedy decisions that made it all effective, you can understand what strengths you have and make use of them later in life too.

6. **Motivate yourself:**

We should stop looking for others to notice how great we did or stop waiting for a round of applause or a pat on the back from them. Instead, we should motivate ourselves every time we fall apart, and we should have the energy to pick ourselves back up again. The feeling of satisfaction we get after completing a task or helping someone, that feeling is what we should strive for. We should become proud of ourselves and our strengths, as well as our weaknesses, that they helped us transform into the person we are today. We should never feel either superior or inferior to others. Everyone has their own pace and their own struggles. Our strengths should not only be for ourselves but for others too. Kindness, empathy, hospitality, being there for people, patience, courage, respect are all the qualities that one must turn into their strengths.

Conclusion:

The key to perfection is self-awareness. There's a fine line between who you are and who you strive to become; it can be achieved by becoming aware of your strengths, polishing them, and creating a sense of professional as well as personal development. Your strengths motivate you to try new things, achieve new skills, become a better version of yourself. Your strengths are what keeps you positive, motivated, help you to maintain your stress better, aid you in your intuitive decision making, and command you to help others as well. It inspires you to become a better person.

Chapter 8:

Seven Habits of Mentally Strong People

Mentally strong people also have great character and charming personalities because they can handle what ordinary people may not handle. Mental strength is the most desired trait by most people. To some, it is innate but others cultivate it over time through education or the school of life. Whichever way it is acquired, there are underlying habits that mentally strong people share.

Here are seven habits of mentally strong people:

1. They Are Forgiving

To err is human but forgiveness is divine. Forgiveness is difficult for most people to commit. It is seen as a sign of weakness but this is a fallacy. The contrary is true. Forgiveness is a measure of strength. When one person grossly transgresses another, the offended party will seek vengeance. He/she feels justified to revenge and until the offender 'pays' for his mistakes, the spirit of the offended will know no rest.

Mentally strong people are capable of forgiveness. This distinguishes them from the rest of the population. They understand that there is no point in re-visiting a matter when they can shelf it and prevent its repeat in the future. It does not mean that the offender has the license to continue hurting the other person. Instead, forgiveness sets the precedence that you are unaffected by the acts of an inconsiderate person. It demonstrates that your reasoning and emotions are not manipulated at will by someone who hurts you.

The next time someone wrongs you, let vengeance take the back seat and reason prevail over your actions. It is what mentally strong people do.

2. They Are Readers

There is nothing new under the sun. Everything that happens is a repetition of something that once occurred. To acquaint yourself with how history judged those who were once in your shoes, flip the pages of books and learn the signs of the time.

The habit of reading is not only for the literate. Even the illiterate can read, not books but the signs of the time and the harsh judgment of history on failures of men. Mentally strong people are wise not to learn from their mistakes but those of others. They unlearn the habits of failures and learn those of the successful.

Readership is a dynamic habit that is perfected by the mentally strong. They read the prevailing situations and adjust their actions accordingly. Reading builds the wealth of experience in life and prepares one on what action to take when confronted by a situation.

3. They Accept Criticism and Correction

Acceptance of correction from an authority displays humility. Correction and positive criticism are not to display your ignorance to the public but instead to inform you on a matter you were once ignorant about. Many people take criticism negatively and want to justify their actions. It is not always about being right or wrong – a concept that most people miss.

Embracing correction distinguishes mentally strong people from the faint-hearted who always rush to justify their acts.

The intelligence of the mentally strong is belittled when they engage in supremacy battles. They rise above the hate and become big brothers/sisters. Only a handful of a population can own up to their misinformation on a matter and humbly accept correction. Mentally strong people can display such levels of maturity.

4. They Are Not Easily Discouraged

It takes a lot to discourage mentally strong people. While ordinary people are stoppable in their tracks, it is not the same for the mentally strong. They are resilient to the adversity of whatever nature. They pursue their targets viciously and settle at nothing short of victory.

Mentally strong people may face a thousand ways to die but survive every one of them. They have the proverbial nine lives of the cat. Their determination is unmatched making them the envy of their peers who give up easily when challenged.

The majority of people in their curriculum vitae say that they can work under pressure. Unfortunately, their breaking point reaches sooner than expected. In the face of immense pressure at work, they yield to frivolous and unrealistic demands meted on them by busybodies. This is not the portion of the mentally strong.

5. They Are Innovative

Mentally strong people are not satisfied with the status quo. They always seek to unsettle the ordinary way of doing things. The traditional handling of affairs does not ogre well with them. There is always a new way of doing things.

Their mental strength is partly responsible for the adventurous spirit. The mentally endowed put their brains to work in solving human problems. They innovate simple life hacks, technology and come up with homemade solutions that were unknown before.

Innovation is not limited to the complicated science of experts. It also involves finding the simplest ways of solving problems in society. Innovation is habitual for mentally strong people.

6. <u>They See The Bigger Picture</u>

Life is a hunt for resources. Similar to the Lion, Mentally strong people do not lose focus of the antelope because of a dashing squirrel. To them, the point of reference is always the bigger picture. They interrogate every matter diligently to read between the lines because the devil always lies in the details.

It is not a matter of the emotions invoked in a discussion but the quality of reasoning devoid of any feelings. Mentally strong people can sieve needs from wants and decant fallacies from discussions.

7. <u>They Are Bold</u>

Fortune favors the bold. It is one thing to be decisive and another to boldly speak out your thoughts. Timidity is for mental infants (no offense). Mentally strong people are not afraid of giving their inputs in forums whenever required to because they speak from a point of knowledge.

The Merry Lady

Fearlessly talking about social ills and injustices is uncommon even among the political class. They lack the mental strength to engage fruitfully in matters of national importance. The bold is unafraid of how they may be challenged by other people because they are capable of seeing everybody's point of view. They appreciate the diversity in opinions.

The above are seven habits of mentally strong people. Mental strength wields untold power to those who possess it.

The Merry Lady

Chapter 9:

5 Scientific Tricks To Become Perfectly Happy

Being happy comes naturally. Almost everything around us makes us happy in a certain way. Being happy is a constant feeling inside a human being. They always tend to get satisfied, even at a minimum. Everywhere we look nowadays, we see things filled with this bright emotion. We tune to the songs written about happiness, we see posters at every corner about being happy, and most importantly, we have people who make us happy. Being happy comes freely, without any fee.

There are scientific ways to become happy because an average human is always looking for more.

Some ways in which you'll feel full at heart and eased at mind. A burst of good laughter is like medicine to the core. So, science has given us ways to take this medicine without and cautions. Being happy is one of the least harmful emotions. It binds people together. Even some forms have been scientifically proven to work in favor of our happiness. There is almost no end to those bright smiles on our lips or those crinkles by our eyes. As it said, smiling is contagious. And we all prefer to smile back at everyone who smiles at us automatically. Here are some scientific ways to be happy.

1. Minutes Into Exercise

It is proven that some exercise helps you to smile and laugh more. If there is an exercise to be happy with, then people would be sure to give it a try now and then. Exercise helps us to regulate our jaw muscle, so it will be easier to pass a smile next time. There is also meditation. It enables you to calm your mind and leads towards an easier life. It usually helps to keep you at peace so you'll feel happier towards the things that should make you happy. You'll start to get more content at certain or small items. It becomes a habit slowly to smile more, be more satisfied. Being happy also benefits others, and then they will be more inclined to be pleased towards you.

2. Get Enough Sleep

Another scientifically proven way to get happy is to sleep enough every night. It helps with the formation of a proper mindset towards your happiness in life. Sleeping at least 8 hours a day is a must for being happy; if not, the 7 hours would suffice enough for you to smile a little more. It keeps your mind and soul at a steady pace, which is inclined to keep us calm and collected. Keeping calm and organized is one of the factors to be happy. Wake up early to listen to the birds or go for a morning run. Keep yourself fresh in the morning to be a better and happier person.

Early to bed is a wise men choice. So, get a sound slumber every night to have a sunny morning following you.

3. Take A Break Now and Then

Even the greatest minds need some rest, so it's only average for a human to get some rest after a long period of working day and night. Go on a vacation. Get a leave because life needs to be enjoyed through anything. Working all the time makes you dull and unhappy. So, make sure to take a break once in a while to start again with a fresh mind and perform a better duty. Don't load yourself with the things that won't matter in a few years. Take vacation so you'll have a more peaceful time ahead of you in your life.

4. Build Your Happy Place

People tend to get tired quickly and often by working all the time. All most of the time, vacation can't seem like an option. So, the best place to visit in such a situation is your happy place—a place you have created in your mind where you are so glad all the time. Just by imagining such a place, you get comfortable and tend to keep working and being pleased with the same time. Your happy place gives you joy, and you become a happier person overall. And it is just easier to carry your vacation with you all the time.

5. Count Your Achievements

A great way to be scientifically happy is to count all the achievements you have made so far. Even count little things like watering plants as an achievement because it gives you a sense of joy. Achievements tell you that you have done more in your life than you intended to, and you will get motivated to do more every time. It makes you believe in yourself and get you going only forwards. You get happy with the deeds you have done till now, and it helps you plan your next good achievement. You naturally become more inclined to fulfill your desires and needs. All the things you have done so far will make you feel beneficial to society and happier for yourself.

Conclusion

Being happy is a great feeling with a more remarkable result in life. So, smiling more won't do you any wrong; in fact, it may be good for you to stretch your jaw a little. Happiness doesn't discriminate, so it will be good to spread this scientific happiness as much as we can. Being happy gives us a sense of undeniable joy and a vision of a positive and bright future.

Chapter 10:

8 Habits That Can Make You Happy

We're always striving for something, whether it's a promotion, a new truck, or anything else. This brings us to an assumption that "when this happens, You'll finally be happy."

While these important events ultimately make us happy, research suggests that this pleasure does not last. A Northwestern University study compared the happiness levels of ordinary people to those who had won the massive lottery in the previous years. It was found that the happiness scores of both groups were nearly equal.

The false belief that significant life events determine your happiness or sorrow is so widespread that psychologists have given it a name- "impact bias." The truth is that event-based happiness is transitory. Satisfaction is artificial; either create it or not. Long term happiness is achieved through several habits. Happy people develop behaviors that keep them satisfied daily.

Here are eight habits that can make you happy.

1. Take Pride in Life's Little Pleasures.

We are prone to falling into routines by nature. This is, in some ways, a positive thing. It helps conserve brainpower while also providing comfort. However, it is possible to be so engrossed in your routine that you neglect to enjoy the little pleasures in life. Happy people understand the value of savoring the taste of their meal, revel in a great discussion they just had, or even simply stepping outside to take a big breath of fresh air.

2. Make Efforts To Be Happy.

Nobody, not even the most ecstatically happy people, wakes up every day feeling this way. They work harder than everyone else. They understand how easy it is to fall into a routine where you don't check your emotions or actively strive to be happy and optimistic. People who are happy continually assess their moods and make decisions with their happiness in mind.

3. Help other people.

Helping others not only makes them happy, but it also makes you happy. Helping others creates a surge of dopamine, oxytocin, and serotonin, all of which generate pleasant sensations. According to Harvard research, people who assist others are ten times more likely to be focused at work and 40% more likely to be promoted. According to the same study, individuals who constantly provide social support are the most likely to be happy during stressful situations. As long as you don't overcommit yourself, helping others will positively affect your mood.

4. Have Deep Conversations.

Happy people understand that happiness and substance go hand in hand. They avoid gossip, trivial conversation, and passing judgment on others. Instead, they emphasize meaningful interactions. You should interact with others on a deeper level because it makes you feel good, creates emotional connections, and, importantly, it's an intriguing way to learn.

5. Get Enough Sleep.

I've pounded this one too hard over the years, and I can't emphasize enough how important sleep is for enhancing your attitude, focus, and self-control. When you sleep, your brain recharges, removing harmful proteins that accumulate as byproducts of regular neuronal activity during the day. This guarantees that you awaken alert and focused. When you don't get enough quality sleep, your energy, attention, and memory all suffer. Even in the absence of a stressor, sleep loss elevates stress hormone levels. Sleep is vital to happy individuals because it makes them feel good, and they know how bad they feel when they don't get enough sleep.

6. Surround yourself with the right people

Happiness is contagious; it spreads through people. Surrounding yourself with happy people boosts your confidence, encourages your creativity, and is simply enjoyable. Spending time with negative people has the opposite effect. They get others to join their self-pity party so that they may feel better about themselves. Consider this: if someone was smoking, would you sit there all afternoon inhaling the second-hand smoke? You'd step back, and you should do the same with negative people.

7. Always Stay Positive.

Everyone, even happy people, encounters difficulties daily. Instead of moaning about how things could or should have been, happy people think about what they are grateful for. Then they find the best approach to the situation, that is, dealing with it and moving on. Pessimism is a powerful source of sadness. Aside from the damaging effects on your mood, the problem with a pessimistic mindset is that it becomes a self-fulfilling prophecy. If you expect bad things, you are more likely to encounter horrific events. Gloomy thoughts are difficult to overcome unless you see how illogical they are. If you force yourself to look at the facts, you'll discover that things aren't nearly as awful as you think.

8. Maintain a Growth Mindset.

People's core attitudes can be classified into two types: fixed mindsets and growth mindsets. You believe you are who you are and cannot change if you have a fixed attitude. When you are challenged, this causes problems because anything that looks to be more than you can handle will make you feel despondent and overwhelmed. People with a growth mindset believe that with effort, they can progress. They are happy as a result of their improved ability to deal with adversity. They also outperform those with a fixed perspective because they welcome difficulties and see them as chances to learn something new.

Conclusion

It can be tough to maintain happiness, but investing your energy in good habits will pay off. Adopting even a couple of the habits on this list will have a significant impact on your mood.